Sp

Who is me?

One of The Katrina Three!

Bonnie Barb Frick

Spookie T. Who Is Me?

One of The Katrina Three!

by
Bonnie Barb Frick

Copyright © 2018 Bonnie Barb Frick
All rights reserved

ISBN-13: 978-1986612418
ISBN-10: 1986612414

Printed in the United States of America
by
CreateSpace, an Amazon.com Company

Available from Amazon.com and other retail outlets

DEDICATION

This book is dedicated to every individual that made the rescue and rehabilitation of The Katrina Three- Big Guy, Spookie T., and Peanut- possible.

ACKNOWLEDGMENTS

Animal rescue agencies and volunteers

Media keeping the public aware of the plight of displaced animals

People who fostered and adopted homeless animals

The public outcry for state and federal officials to create regulations for future disasters

Passage of the Pet Evacuation and Transportation Standards (PETS) Act

CONTENTS

Introduction	9
At the Top of Green Street Hill	15
Today	15
Days Later	17
Weeks Later	19
More Weeks Later	23
Owners Vacation with The Guest in Location	30
Home Sweet Home	37
Fair and Balanced	38
In Memoriam: Peanut	41
Incognito: Big Guy	43
In the Middle: Spookie T.	46
Months Later	49
I Lost My Brother	52
Big Guy: The King	55
Spookie T., Feliner	58

SPOOKIE T. WHO IS ME?
ONE OF THE KATRINA THREE!

INTRODUCTION

The rain poured! The floodwaters rose! The winds gusted! Terrified, The Katrina Three sought shelter. Bracing himself against the swirling winds and the pelting rain, the big brother motioned to his brother and sister to follow him. The Three survived the storm. Now, what?

Rescued from the Mississippi Gulf Coast, they snared a corner in the makeshift shelter where rescuers had carefully delivered them. Barks, meows, and howls filled the room. Lost, alone, and frightened, the three kittens were relieved to be housed, dry, fed, and, more importantly, still together as a family.

Hurricane Katrina is one of the deadliest and most expensive natural disasters in United States history. From August 23-31, 2005, Katrina caused 1,833 deaths and $125 billion damage. New Orleans, Louisiana, and the Mississippi Gulf Coast were among the areas most severely affected.

On August 29, Hurricane Katrina made landfall on the Gulf Coast of Mississippi, leaving 238 people dead and causing massive damage. The impact of landfall near the mouth of the Pearl River slammed the Coast, causing a storm surge more than 26 feet high in coastal cities, devastating structures along the beachfront. Populated areas of Harrison, Hancock, and Jackson counties were inundated. Reportedly, surges traveled as far as six miles inland on parts of the Mississippi Coast. Katrina also spawned eleven tornadoes in the state on that day. Battered by wind, rain, and storm surge, a total of 65,000 homes were destroyed in Mississippi, leaving more than 100,000 people homeless.

Meanwhile, thousands of volunteers descended onto the Gulf Coast to join local and national animal agencies attempting to rescue thousands of animals. Many nonhuman family members had been left behind to fend for themselves because official disaster response had no provision for the evacuation of pets along with their families. Some residents absolutely refused to leave without their pets. The significance of pets being disposable property outraged this nation of animal lovers, including some powerful members of Congress.

The public flooded Congress with letters. Despite being politically divided over immigration, war, and other issues, in 2006 Congress passed—with almost unanimous support—the Pet Evacuation and Transportation Standards (PETS) Act requiring local jurisdictions to have pet evacuation plans in place to qualify for federal funding in the event of a disaster. The PETS Act, a law that compels rescue agencies to save pets as well as people during natural disasters, has saved countless animal lives in subsequent disasters.

Once wild creatures, twenty-first century pets have become family members in their homes and in the eyes of the law during natural disasters. Hurricane Katrina was a landmark moment for pets in American history. For the first time, lawmakers determined that during natural disasters, pets should be treated like people.

Hurricane Katrina was also a landmark moment for three Siamese kittens living in the coastal area of Mississippi. Katrina arrived. Their owners departed. The three kittens were left to weather the storm on their own. And they did with a little help from new friends.

These three little kittens had lost their owners, and two began to cry, "Oh, Brother Dear, what should we do?"

He answered, "I don't know," with a sigh.

In time, one of those thousands descending

onto the Gulf Coast to join local and national agencies attempting to rescue animals left behind found three wet, hungry, frightened, part-Siamese kittens. The rescuers probably found it hard to believe that these three were indeed siblings. One looked very Siamese. One looked somewhat Siamese. The gray one with yellow eyes looked barely Siamese.

The three kittens were rescued and sheltered together, but no one came to claim them. As requests for adoptions circulated throughout the country, a family from Maryland adopted The Three. After eight years of living, hiding, and adjusting in a two-story home with their loving new owners, The Three and their family moved to a one-story villa in Pennsylvania. The Three, of course, found the complexities of moving difficult.

Now, more than a decade after Hurricane Katrina, Spookie T(he). Cat, middle one of

The Katrina Three, invites you to share his reminiscences about life as a Katrina rescue.

The Katrina Three Plus One

Big Guy	King	Respected	Aloof
Spookie T.	Jester	Tolerated	Goofy
Peanut	Princess	Coddled	Dependent
The Guest	Caretaker	Trusted	Familial

AT THE TOP OF GREEN STREET HILL

TODAY

Perched high above Route 222 and at the top of Green Street Hill is a villa-a reflection of eight villas farther down the hill. Unlike its neighbors, this villa is wrapped in a cloud of privacy. The secluded side entrance and a tall wooden fence located by spreading conifers complement the villa's mystique.

Within, a male cat gazes out the patio door from atop his personal perch. He watches birds fly to the woods, trees list in the wind, and leaves skip across the lawn. He is involved. He is safe. He is content. He is home. Returning from his reverie, Big Guy jumps down, going in pursuit of his two siblings.

Moments later, he joins his brother Spookie T. and sister Peanut under the bed in the room where the two have been napping. He says, "We are so fortunate. We have experienced several traumatic events, especially Hurricane Katrina. We are still together and living securely and comfortably here at the top of Green Street Hill." Spookie T. and Peanut quietly purr assent and snuggle against their strong, loving brother before the three float into dreamland-together, comfortable, and safe.

DAYS LATER

A few days later, The Guest, their personal cat sitter, chats at the kitchen island with their owner. Spookie T. and Big Guy find this unsettling. They never appear when visitors are near. Little Peanut has courageously moved from under the bed to under the covers to high atop the very bed pillows her brothers consider theirs.

Nonplussed, Big Guy leaves the bedroom and ventures into the dining room. "Hmm," he thinks, "The Guest is here. I wonder why." Before he can investigate, Spookie T. joins his big brother. They exchange glances before Big Guy walks over to The Guest and sniffs her hand. "No treats!" After circling the room, Big Guy recaptures his friendly genes and returns to recheck the situation. "No treats! How could she? She always gives me treats if I leave the bedroom. Oh, well, it's not going to work today."

Meanwhile, Spookie T. watches Big Guy from a distance, understanding the message. "It doesn't matter anyway," he thinks. "Big Guy beats me to the treats most times unless The Guest throws his treats in one direction and mine in another."

The brothers eventually leave the dining room to return to the comfort of the bedroom. The Guest says, "Wow, how far they have come! They seem to be somewhat relaxed in my presence." Their owner agrees and smiles with appreciation for their actions.

WEEKS LATER

Weeks later, "MEOW!" Big Guy howls. Spookie T. keeps moving. Peanut disappears into the paint on the wall under the bed. Something big-really big-is happening.

A hint of trauma slowly spreads throughout the villa as lots of water makes its way from the roof into the bedroom. The Three hear telephone conversations, see strange males, and hear heavy footsteps moving throughout the house. The men keep entering and exiting the villa.

Furniture appears in different locations. Cardboard and plastic cover the walkways. The more the busyness increases, the longer and tighter Big Guy and his siblings huddle under the bed. The Three can hear and see, but they cannot understand. All they know is that they are experiencing that Katrina Feeling again and are not, indeed, as safe as they have believed.

The room is no longer their safe haven. Food dishes and a litter box appear. Their owners move into the room, too, as loud roaring comes from the bedroom. Their world appears to be falling apart, and their home could be disappearing-again. As Peanut huddles closer than close to the wall, Big Guy and Spookie T. feel their muscles tighten. Big Guy again takes command and tries to be the best big brother he can be as the little brother inside him keeps surfacing.

Days later, with the fans still running, Spookie T. is close to panic. "How many days can I hold on? I just want to hide in a closet until whatever is going on is over. Will it ever be over? Time seems to be going so slowly."

Tension reigns within the villa. Multiple workers invade its privacy. The garage door goes up and down, up and down. The doors open and close, open and close.

And then—silence. Silence that comes from the absence of roaring fans. Spookie T. snaps awake, listens, and smiles. "The fans have stopped! Maybe normalcy can return. Maybe normalcy will return." Although many different sounds replace the continuous roaring of the fans, the house appears to be nearing its former condition. How many more days will the restoration from the flooding take? Spookie T. determines whatever amount of time it takes, the villa at the top of Green Street is on its way to becoming wrapped in privacy again. "Oh, what a relief!" he thinks.

With the feeling of trauma waning, Spookie T. shares his feelings with Big Guy and Peanut. Big Guy agrees, but Peanut is not convinced. Her brothers exchange knowing glances. It will take time, but they will work to help Peanut get through and over yet another traumatic experience. They realize that each of them has part of that same journey to make themselves.

A wave of peace floats through the room as the three allow themselves to relax a bit and to look forward to better days ahead. Sleep arrives, bringing with it feline dreams.

MORE WEEKS LATER

"Meow! MEow! MEOw! MEOW!"

"What is going on, Spookie T.?"

"That's what I want to know, Big Guy. What's going on around here?"

"What are you talking about? I was just in the middle of a beautiful dream when you started caterwauling. Try not to wake Peanut up."

"Wake Peanut up? What are you talking about? She's lying against the wall under the bed with her eyes wide open and staring at you, waiting to hear what you have to say."

"What I have to say about what, Spookie T.?"

"What you have to say about what is going on around here."

"I don't have anything to say about what's going on around here since the fans and the men are gone. It's the first decent sleep I've had."

"Big Guy, are you awake or not?"

"I'm wide awake now, but I don't know why."

"Haven't you noticed something missing around here?"

"Something? What something?"

"Dad!"

"Dad?"

"Yes, Dad," Peanut says quietly.

"What are you two talking about?"

"Dad has not slept in this house for two nights," Spookie T. explains.

"Why hasn't he slept here?" Big Guy asks.

"That's what we want to know from you, Big Brother."

"How should I know? The dishes are filled, the boxes are cleaned, and The Guest isn't coming and going, so . . . . You're right, Spookie T. With all the hubbub around here and so many workmen's shoes coming and going, I haven't noticed that the shoes with the orange trim have been missing."

"Are you an idiot? On whose side of the bed do you usually sleep at night?"

"Oh, Spookie T., I have been so tired that I haven't even attempted to jump onto the bed to sleep next to Dad. Oh, I feel terrible."

"Well, Big Guy, not only has he not slept here, but also The Guest hasn't been here. Mom has been taking care of us, but she is now doing something really weird."

"Really weird?"

"Yes, really weird."

"Yes, it's really weird that she isn't away with Dad, but maybe he had to return to the hospital."

"Good thought, Big Guy, but I'm not sure that is the case."

"Why not?"

"Go look at what she's doing. Maybe then you'll start wondering what's going on around here."

"What's she doing, Spookie T.?"

"I said, 'Go look.' Now, go look!"

Big Guy returns and asks, "Has Peanut seen what Mom's doing?"

"No, I have tried to act natural to make sure she doesn't suddenly peel herself off the wall and leave the room."

"Good job, Spookie T. Thanks for stepping in for me. What do you think is going on around here?"

"You tell me. I don't know or even want to know. It doesn't look good. I'm not feeling very secure right now."

"Spookie T., there has got to be an explanation for what's going on around here. We cannot allow ourselves to jump to conclusions after all these years."

"I agree, Big Guy, but Peanut and I can think of no good explanation."

"Mom is an artist."

"Yes."

"Maybe she started painting again now that we're moved and settled in."

"Big Guy, I repeat, 'Are you an idiot?' Why would anyone return to something so creative in the middle of this craziness caused by the gigantic leak in the bedroom? Why? To pass time?"

"Well, that answer does not sound plausible. What other reason is there?"

"What is she painting?"

"Spookie T., she's painting the portrait of a strange man! A strange man when Dad's not here. Spookie T., what should we do?"

"Wait to see what happens," Peanut says quietly.

Both brothers turn with a start and stare at their sister with eyes and mouths open wide and say, "What? Wait?"

"You two are so male. You can't fix what you don't know is wrong," Peanut quietly declares.

"Yes, true, Peanut, but we have to do something."

"Big Guy," Peanut says, "let's trust our owners and wait to see what happens before panicking."

"*Trust*. That's a good word, *trust*," Big Guy says as Spookie T.'s head starts bobbing up and down.

Spookie T. asks, "How long should we wait?"

Big Guy says, "Until we're more sure of what's going on around here."

"That could be days or even weeks. I think I'm going to go hide in Mom's closet. See you two later."

Big Guy, Spookie T., and Peanut have no way of knowing that they must wait another night and well into the next day before they find out what's going on around there.

While The Three continue trusting and waiting to see what happens, they hear the garage door going up.

"Oh, not another workman," Big Guy says as the door from the garage into the hallway opens. Then they hear Dad say, "Hello," and see Mom go to greet him.

"That's a good sign," Big Guy declares.

"Yes," says Spookie T., who has finally come out of the closet. "What is Dad saying? I can't quite hear him."

Big Guy says, "I can't hear everything either."

Peanut looks up and says, "He said, 'I'm glad to be home from the funeral in California. How's the portrait of your doctor friend going?'"

Unheard by Dad and Mom are three short, quiet sighs of relief.

Peanut sits quietly and thinks, "I told you so, Guys."

OWNERS VACATION

WITH THE GUEST IN LOCATION

Thursday Evening

    The Guest arrives; The Three sigh.

    Directions read; cats to be fed.

    Chores completed; felines treated.

    Nurturing aside; The Guest says, "Bye."

    Ready to leave; checks the laundry.

    A mound of litter; odor worse than liver.

Friday Morning

    Spookie T. awakened, remained unshaken.

    Closeted to hide; Big Guy arrived.

    Peanut alert; relaxed little squirt.

Friday Evening

    Fun and games; males not tame.

    Chasing one another; Spookie T. doesn't holler

when hitting something, running without looking.

They play; The Guest stays.

Big Guy stares; Spookie T. cares.

Cannot tempt him to let her pet him.

Goes behind the chair; feeling safe there.

The guys pacing; waiting for racing.

Saturday Morning

Shhh! Sleeping; Spookie T.'s peeping

from atop his pillow, feeling mellow.

Peanut-love her; Big Guy's covered,

not even a move when hearing food.

All in place in their spaces.

Quiet night; two toys took flight.

Food devoured; parting hour.

Little news, not even mews.

All is calm-until The Guest is gone.

Saturday Evening

Big Guy eats as The Guest repeats.

Two males moving; Peanut proving

she can sit and smile a long, long while,

not desiring a friend to play and pretend.

Spookie T. rodeos from the studio.

Big Guy rests, seated at Mom's desk.

Game players supreme; wish owners had seen.

Sunday Morning

Betwixt and between, what an interesting scene!

Later, will get back to the facts about that.

Spookie T. arrives; Big Guy likewise.

Then each departs, making claws sharp.

Back and forth, sometimes a bit rough,

the brothers race around the place.

Water running; the dishes scrubbing.

The Guest belongs; the males play strong.

The two are fine; it's boys' playtime.

The boys seem to be unaffected by her company.

Chores completed; boys to be treated.

Relaxed, both wait for their respective bait.

Each eating a bunch; neither wanting to be touched.

Normalcy feels good at 7:00 in the 'hood.

All's quiet and serene; hate leaving the scene.

Must get ready for church; can't leave spouse in a lurch.

Counting time arrives; The Guest's in for a surprise.

Peanut's missing; could arouse no hissing.

Saw her sweat when not finding third pet.

Flashlight in hand, went everywhere to scan.

Calling her name, asked Big Guy to explain,

searching every room, with flashlight to zoom.

Twice around; no Peanut found.

Upon request, Big Guy no help The Guest.

Determined, with a slouch, she rechecks the couch.

Between wall and couch squeezed, she searches with unease.

She squeezes a bit more, hearing something like snores.

No cat to be seen; she squeezes farther between,

determined to move, determined to prove

Peanut was there as Big Guy stared,

attempting to distract The Guest from the track.

One shove, and wow; a flying cat yowls,

runs to her brother, her loyal cover.

The Three comfortably rest under the bed's dress.

They've made her sweat and will again, she bets.

Sunday Evening

The Guest comes inside; Boys go outside.

Peanut content under wooden tent.

Big Guy eats; Spookie T. retreats.

Snacks provided; Peanut still hidin'.

Time to depart–Peanut warms The Guest's heart.

Standing in the doorway, staring her way.

She then lies down, not a trace of a frown.

She curls her paws up under her jaws.

She responds to her name, plays no cat games.

Many minutes pass; she leaves, alas.

Wow! What a surprise! She's made such strides.

What a treasure! Cannot be measured.

She thanks God for Peanut's nod.

Monday Morning

Hi, Guys! No surprises.

Some toys scattered; nothing mattered.

Gets to the dishes-fulfilled her wishes.

There, The Three staring at she.

The Guest stands in wonder, talking as she ponders.

Big Guy waiting; Spookie T. awakening.

Peanut staring; conversation sharing.

Minutes mount; cannot count.

Would stand for hours, but must shower.

She's an amazing creature. She wants to reach her.

Time to leave; count The Three.

In their spaces with calm faces.

The Guest shall go, wearing a glow.

HOME SWEET HOME

Home, sweet home.

Their owners gone,

The Three adjust

and grow in trust.

The Three have grown

to be alone

without concern

for owners' return.

THE GUEST'S SONG

A corrupted song comes to mind:

This is the way to scoop the poop,

scoop the poop, scoop the poop.

This is the way to scoop the poop

early Monday morning.

FAIR AND BALANCED?

Sitting alone, watching television, Little Peanut reflects–no one is home. Why's TV on? Curious, Little Peanut watches what's on, currently Fox News–Fair and Balanced. (Come on!)

Bedroom-bound, self-inflicted, Little Peanut's brothers sharing, conflicted. Nobody's home. TV's on. Little Peanut's on her own. Ordinary's gone. Brothers moan, silence returns. Sister groans. Feline conversation interrupts Little Peanut's concentration.

Back to the news. Little Peanut's amused–changes of scenes, flashes of light, loud commercials–her muses. Brothers safely, nervously hide together, darkness surrounding. TV's on. Nobody's home. She's on her own. Ordinary's gone. Little Peanut continues watching light flood the screen, the room, erasing her gloom.

Fox News: Flooding takes lives. Hearing the word *flooding* widens Little Peanut's eyes. No surprise. Flooding, no matter the size, starts from the sky, being part of strife filling The Three's lives. Just last month, their lives compromised again: rain falling, icicles growing, water pouring, workmen repairing, noises unending–three felines hiding to survive.

"We survived," Little Peanut thinks. Wind, rain, flooding. Soaked carpet, ceiling, walls. Men wearing coveralls. Did hiding, darkness, fear help us survive?

A jolt of lightning fills Little Peanut's brain. All this light. Ordinary changed. Fox news, outdoor views, her muse fills the dark with startling sight. Hiding is not right, causes loss of might. Together, we three must fight for right, recapture our might. Ordinary is ordinary including plight. Fright, their choice, replacing temporary flight from the site.

Meowing with insight, insistent to share, Little Peanut marches into the bedroom, confronting the pair, "We must fight for the right of our might!"

Shaking sleep away, together they say, "For the right of our might we must fight?" What's Little Peanut mean—might, fight, right?

Explaining her visionary insight, Little Peanut stands facing her two bigger brothers, "Tonight is the night my fight begins, regaining my feline might!"

Big Guy, Spookie T. confused lie pondering what Little Peanut relates. Marching toward the light, Little Peanut states, "Let me know when considering fighting for the right of your might." What else could she say to brothers avoiding light of day, joy of play, life fair and balanced?

IN MEMORIAM: PEANUT

A heart-filled Peanut living in a deteriorating shell,

Fighting for life, which eventually became hell.

In her two years living at the top of the Hill,

Her quest for life provided thrill upon thrill.

Once hidden, untouchable, protected by her brothers,

Peanut wasn't inclined to be vulnerable to others.

The strength of her desire to be one of the family

Motivated her progression from obscurity to reality.

Having chosen to live within public view,

Miss Peanut experienced pleasure and energy anew.

She was a cat, not a recluse as had been thought,

Overtly staring or departing uncaught.

For one whose life had been plagued by trauma

But yet chose vulnerability and feline drama,

Being woman is what she determined to be,

And within two years achieved it successfully.

Now living in a pain-free, peaceful place,

Miss Peanut is oblivious to time and space.

But in our hearts, we can hear her sing

Lyrics to a song that carry a sting.

> I am woman, hear me roar
> In numbers too big to ignore.

> Oh yes, I am wise
> But it's wisdom born of pain
> Yes, I've paid the price
> But look how much I gained
> If I have to, I can do anything
> I am strong
> I am invincible
> I am woman.

INCOGNITO: BIG GUY

What someone sees is not what someone gets.
The real B. G.-unrevealed yet.
Perfect posture, strong feline lines,
good imposter, oh so many times.

Young and dependent suddenly disappeared
like Mother when Katrina finally cleared.
Smacked with authority and responsibility
for making his two siblings safe and comfortable.

Acting calm, cool, collected,
not wanting accidentally to be neglected.
Only the courage of a young lion
kept The Three waifs from dyin'.

With head held high and shoulders straight,
he lets no one superficially mistake
the strength and confidence of the leader
currying refuge among displaced critters.

The act worked; A king was born,

never again to endure scorn.

Captured, nurtured, eventually adopted,

The kitten gone; long live the adapted!

Growing up overnight, responsible for siblings-

to a kitten's life-absolutely crippling.

Living comfortably shrouded in fear,

overwhelms as old age comes near.

Looking back, reality attacks;

Being King Incognito not a life-long act.

Peanut gone; Spookie T. strong;

Continuing to cover fear feels wrong.

Wrong? Someone misunderstanding might ask.

Being Incognito's a strenuous task.

Living simultaneously in two worlds-opposite

for a senior feline-a life unfit.

Conditioning and adaptation, both powerful,

making life for the Royal One sorrowful.

Adjusting to another home by owners picked

demonstrates an old feline CAN learn new tricks.

What is seen is not what's gotten.

Aging and dependence slowly begotten.

Revelation, a decade in arriving,

becomes the new vehicle for surviving.

Who needs the most assuring strokes?

Who misses his vacationing folks?

Who hides under the bed in his room?

Who cowers in fear during thunderstorms?

IN THE MIDDLE: SPOOKIE T.

Life in the middle is not easy.
    It's not what it's expected to be.
    An older brother and a younger sister
    are somewhat important to consider.

Being seen but not heard–an unfavorability.
    Protective bookends is a possibility.
    Ignoring the middle a probability.
    Being included an improbability.

Meet Spookie T., the one in the middle unseen,
    suffering from being in between.
    Peanut, the baby, traumatized.
    Big Guy, the elder, most recognized.

The one in the middle alone.
    Rescued as siblings needing a home.
    Baby, Middle, and Elder met trauma.
    Trapped in a hurricane, lost Momma.

The one in the middle, unseen.
>   Traumatized, homeless, rescued three.
>   How wonderful this could be!
>   Lacking equality for Spookie T.

Feline in the Middle, not a fun game,
>   especially when appearances aren't the same.
>   Spookie T., gray with yellow eyes,
>   understands his position sans surprise.

Recognized as the one in the middle,
>   becomes visible, accepted, cuddled.
>   Time passes; changes arrive,
>   Spookie T. still gray with yellow eyes.

He peacefully sleeps in the middle
>   after time to cuddle.
>   Loneliness and desire for brotherly play
>   have been gently, carefully rubbed away.

He sleeps, not the sleep of the dead,

 but the sleep of a soul found before death.

 Still unsure of life and its storms,

 he hesitantly gives into Her charms.

Feeling comfort tail to head,

 Curled in a ball on the bed.

 If he believes the change permanent,

 he'll stretch his legs in contentment.

Even breathing and a sigh or two,

 an invisible feline comes into view.

 His sister and brother–both Siamese.

 Spookie T., the one no one sees.

MONTHS LATER

With Tuesday evening's visit by The Guest over, the Boys leave their den under the bed to refresh themselves and to plan the evening's activities. Although they vowed not to play chase anymore, they had several other activities planned for the evening that they felt would be their last night alone-so to speak.

"You know, Spookie T., it's been fun living without the appearance of an authority figure. We've been free to discover a bit more about a life of freedom from fear. Hurricane Katrina is years gone, and here we are in charge of our home."

"B. G., I think Peanut figured that out well before her big, protective brothers have. She stopped hiding. She interacted with people she liked being around. She lived life before her passing. What a wonderful witness to her siblings!"

"Oh, Spookie T., I think we might have been a bit overprotective, especially me. I put on a strong face, took care of my brother and sister, and, in so doing, denied myself the opportunity to get over IT."

"B. G., don't be so hard on yourself. I took the easier route of letting you take care of us and playing the role of a goofball. Just like you, I am afraid of storms, but not as much as I once was because playing goofball allowed me to see my fears were not realistic. Also, my dear brother, like Peanut, I've faced a life-changing time of poor health that reminded me that life is to be lived- lived just as Peanut eventually learned."

"Spookie T., you know that anything that comes near to being like a hurricane now throws me into panic. I don't like it, but I find I'm more fearful each time."

Moving toward B. G., licking the back of his head, and intertwining their heads, Spookie T.

whispered, "I understand. You are only now beginning to let what has been trapped within you be viewed by your loved ones. Trust me to help you learn to live life, too. I love you."

Following a few quiet moments, two tails rose and formed a heart as Spookie T. suggested, "Let's party! First, we'll play hide-n-seek and then we'll rug dance—my treat."

I LOST MY BROTHER (2018)

I lost my brother today;

I cannot find him anyway.

    I've checked in Mom's closet.

    I've checked the Studio.

    I've checked under the couch.

        He's nowhere to be found.

        He usually makes no sound.

        He last was lying around,

        Wearing a pain-filled frown.

I lost my brother today;

I cannot find him anyway.

    I've checked in Dad's closet.

    I've checked the laundry room.

    I've checked under the bed.

I'm lonely without him.

He's always been my play friend,

Participating the best he can.

Is he playing hide 'n seek again?

I lost my brother yesterday;

I cannot find him anyway.

I've checked the boxes.

I've checked the stands.

I've checked the porch.

He's nowhere to be found.

He did make some odd sounds.

He made no sleeping mound.

He's always, always around.

I lost my brother yesterday.

I cannot understand what they say.

I've checked their faces.

I've checked more spaces.

I'm left with limited choices.

    I'm beginning to understand–

    My brother got lost by plan.

    He's no longer part of our clan.

    My bother's gone: I'm the man.

I've lost my brother, I understand.

Some illness shortened his life span.

    He's not to be found.

    He'll not make a sound.

    He lies peacefully in the ground.

    My understanding's not complete.

    My checking places will repeat.

    My loneliness is oh so deep.

    My hill to climb so very steep.

I've lost my brother–forever.   ~Spookie T.

BIG GUY: THE KING

The King is dead.

Long live his memory.

Definitely a blue blood

with a demeanor to match.

Being a Katrina rescue,

he remained a bit detached.

Head of his feline family,

a position he accepted.

With unyielding caring,

his family protected.

In his home at 310,

Big Guy learned new tricks:

how to welcome The Guest

and greet her as a pick.

Learned not to steal treats

and to wait for his turn

with praise and commendation,

prizes he would earn.

With his head held high

and his perfect posture,

his tail in the air—

worthy of an Oscar.

For when thunder accompanied

by loud winds and lightning

stormed around his home,

he found them frightening.

He trilled, he chirped,

he yowled, he purred—

a talented Siamese,

he preferred being unheard.

Big Guy,

one of a kind—

for his sister he pined,

thought his brother just fine.

Maintained responsibility,

displayed agility,

offered agreeability,

retired with immobility.

The King is dead.

Long live his memory.

SPOOKIE T., FELINER

Author and cattoonist, Spookie T. is a locally known feliner recognized for his expertise in working with cats suffering from Katrinaosis. Like the doctors in a MASH unit, Spookie T. uses humor to remove the sting of pathos when working with his patients. They arrive. They love. They depart.

"I am now an only cat, a new, uncomfortable role that I neither expected nor desired. Like President Truman's wife Bess, it's a role I am bound to accept. I guess an old cat can learn new tricks. At age 12, I have become pet master of the house, a lonely position with lots of benefits."

BONNIE BARB FRICK

Bonnie Barb Frick is a retired high school English teacher. With the birth of her grandchildren, she turned from writing poetry to writing books for her grandson and granddaughter, early readers. This former road not taken started with an autobiography, picture books, and stories to be read aloud. Chapter books followed with Chip and Chirp, two imaginary dove friends, taking up residence in her brain and becoming the storytellers for three children's books: *Chip and Chirp Tell Stories of Jesus, Birds' Eye Views of Historic Downtown Lancaster (PA), Chip and Chirp Tell Presidential Tales.*

Taking care of three Hurricane Katrina cats adopted by neighbors pointed her in the direction of her next chapter book about Spookie T. and his two siblings. Her experiences being Caretaker for The Three provided an opportunity to teach about history, helping others, life's ups and downs, and family. In short-faith, hope, and charity.

Made in the USA
Columbia, SC
26 March 2018